W9-BFN-225

LIGHTNING BOLT BOOKS™

How Do Hot Air Balloons Work?

Buffy Silverman

Lerner Publications Company
Minneapolis

To Jake,
Thanks for the
dandelions!

Lerner Publications Company
A division of Lerner Publishing Group, Inc.
241 First Avenue North
Minneapolis, MN 55401 U.S.A.

Website address: www.lernerbooks.com

Library of Congress Cataloging-in-Publication Data

Silverman, Buffy.
    How do hot air balloons work? / Buffy Silverman.
      p.   cm. — (Lightning bolt books™—How flight works)
    Includes index.
    ISBN 978–0–7613–8969–9 (lib. bdg. : alk. paper)
    1. Hot air balloons—Juvenile literature. 2. Ballooning—Juvenile literature. I. Title.
  TL638.S55 2013
    629.133'22—dc23   2012010394

Manufactured in the United States of America
1 — MG — 12/31/12

Table of Contents

Going Up

A hot air balloon rises on a clear morning.

A light breeze
pushes it in the sky.

What makes a balloon go up? Hot air! Hot air is lighter than cool air. It rises and pushes a balloon up.

Hot air makes this balloon fly high.

The pilot turns on a burner. The burner sits under the envelope. That's the big cloth bag shaped like a balloon.

This is the envelope. The burner is underneath it.

The burner makes a flame. The flame shoots up. It reaches the skirt. That's the bottom part of the envelope. The skirt is made of fabric that will not burn.

The flame heats the air around it. **The warmer air rises into the envelope and lifts the balloon.**

Warm air lets this balloon take off.

The colorful envelope is huge! It must hold enough hot air to lift people and the balloon.

The envelope is strong and light. Wind does not rip it.

In the Basket

From the basket, people can see in all directions. Often three to five people ride inside. Large baskets hold fifteen people or more.

The view from this balloon is amazing!

The basket also holds fuel tanks. Hoses bring fuel to the burner.

The pilot turns a knob called a valve to let more fuel flow to the burner. The flame grows larger. It makes more heat and pushes the balloon up faster.

Pilots control how fast a balloon rises.

How can a pilot slow a rising balloon? He lets hot air out of an opening near the top. The opening is called a vent.

All balloons have a vent near the top.

Cords run down from the vent.
They connect to a single
control cord. The pilot pulls
on the cord. The vent
opens, and
hot air
escapes.

This is the
control cord.

The air in the envelope cools with the vent open. The cool air makes the balloon heavier. It starts to sink.

This balloon is headed downward.

Following the Wind

When you ride a bicycle, you steer it to go where you want. A balloon pilot cannot do that.

Balloons cannot be steered.

Hot air balloons
drift where
the wind blows.
They float
like dandelion
seeds on a
breezy day.

Have you ever
seen dandelion
seeds blow? Hot
air balloons float
the same way.

But a pilot has some control of a balloon. Before a pilot flies, she gets a weather report. She finds out the direction of the wind and the wind speed.

Weather reports help balloon pilots.

Watch clouds on a windy day. Which direction are they blowing? High clouds blow in one direction. Low clouds blow in another direction. Some move faster than others.

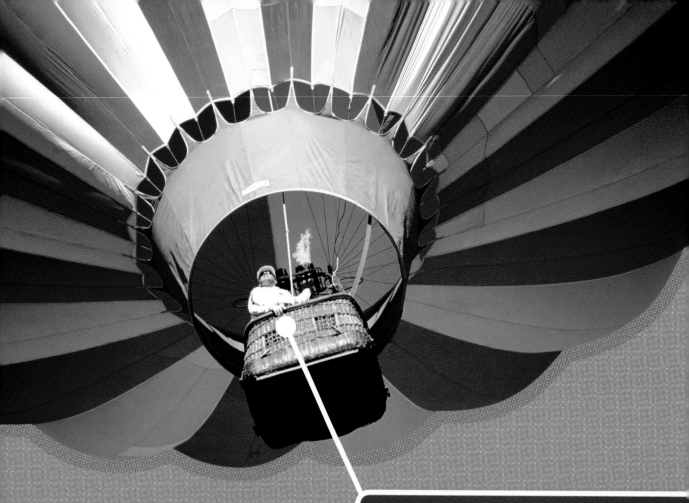

Pilots can move their balloons up or down to catch winds that are blowing in a certain direction.

Wind blows in different directions at different heights. It also moves at different speeds. As the balloon goes higher, the wind moves faster.

An altimeter tells the pilot
how high the balloon is.
The pilot can go higher if he
wants to go faster.

This is an
altimeter.

Floating Down

A pilot looks for an open field. There the balloon can come down safely.

This field is a great landing place!

A truck follows the balloon as it flies. The pilot radios the crew in the truck. He tells them where the balloon is going.

This truck is following a hot air balloon.

The pilot turns the knob that shuts off the fuel. The burner stops. The air in the envelope starts to cool.

This pilot is preparing to land the balloon.

The pilot pulls on the cord to open the vent. Hot air goes out of the top of the balloon. Cooler air flows in from the bottom. **The balloon goes down.**

The balloon is now heavier than the air. It drops closer and closer to the ground.

Bump! It lands in a field. The basket tilts to one side. The passengers climb out.

The crew packs up the balloon. The passengers climb inside the truck. The balloon ride is over.

This crew packs up a balloon.

Hot Air Balloon Diagram

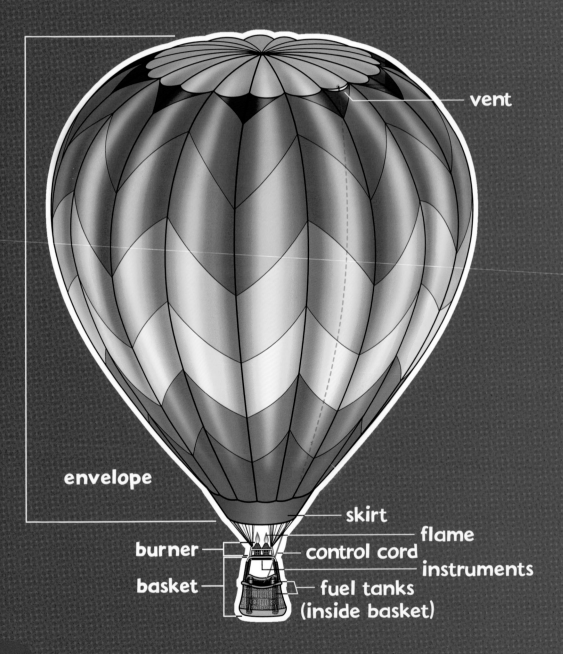

vent

envelope

skirt

flame

burner

control cord

instruments

basket

fuel tanks
(inside basket)

Fun Facts

- Two brothers in France built the first hot air balloon. They experimented with fire and silk bags. The bags rose when filled with air heated by fire. The brothers didn't understand why this was so. But it gave them the idea to build their balloon.

- The first hot air balloon flight took place in 1783. The brothers who built the first balloon sent a sheep, a duck, and a chicken up in their machine! They had promised their dad they wouldn't fly in the balloon themselves.

- The first human flight took place two months after the animals went up. A scientist and an army major rode in the balloon. The flight was a success!

- These days, hot air balloon festivals occur all over the world. The largest one is in New Mexico. About 750 balloons fly in it.

Glossary

altimeter: an instrument for measuring how high a hot air balloon is

burner: a fuel-burning device that produces a flame and heat

envelope: a cloth bag that holds in hot air in a hot air balloon

skirt: the bottom part of a hot air balloon's envelope

valve: a movable part that controls the flow of gas or liquid

vent: an opening in a hot air balloon that lets hot air escape

Further Reading

Dragonfly TV: The Great Balloon Race
http://pbskids.org/dragonflytv/games/game_balloon.html

Dragonfly TV: Hot Air Balloons
http://pbskids.org/dragonflytv/show/balloon.html

Priceman, Marjorie. *Hot Air: The (Mostly) True Story of the First Hot-Air Balloon Ride.* New York: Atheneum Books for Young Readers, 2005.

Rau, Dana Meachen. *Hot Air Balloons.* New York: Marshall Cavendish Benchmark, 2011.

Science Kids: Warm Air Needs More Room
http://www.sciencekids.co.nz/experiments/heavyair.html

Silverman, Buffy. *How Do Jets Work?* Minneapolis: Lerner Publications Company, 2013.

Index

Photo Acknowledgments

The images in this book are used with the permission of: © Susan Isakson/age fotostock/SuperStock, p. 1; © NightOwl/Shutterstock.com, p. 2; ©iStockphoto.com/Ivan Cholakov, p. 4; © Steve Vidler/SuperStock, pp. 5, 7; © JCREATION/Shutterstock.com, p. 6; © iStockphoto.com/ElementalImaging, p. 8; © Tom Brakefield/SuperStock, p. 9; © Konrad Wothe/LOOK Die Bildagentur der Fotografen GmbH/Alamy, p. 10; © mikeledray/Shutterstock.com, p. 11; © William Henley/Alamy, p. 12; David Wall/DanitaDelimont.com/Newscom, p. 13; © Kumar Sriskandan/Alamy, p. 14; © Samuel Acosta/Shutterstock.com, p. 15; © G. Brad Lewis/Science Faction/CORBIS, p. 16; © JanBussan/Shutterstock.com, p. 17; © Image Source/Alamy, p. 18; © Thierry Maffeis/Shutterstock.com, p. 19; © Nordic Photos/SuperStock, p. 20; © Denise Hager/Catchlight Visual Services/Alamy, p. 21; © Eddie Hironaka/Photographer's Choice/Getty Images, p. 22; © Massimo Dallaglio/Alamy, p. 23; AP Photo/Jose F. Moreno, p. 24; © iStockphoto.com/Stephan Hoerold, p. 25; © Sunpix Travel/Alamy, p. 26; © Lightworks Media/Alamy, p. 27; © Laura Westlund/Independent Picture Service, p. 28; © iStockphoto.com/Michael Flippo, p. 30, © Jim Lozouski/Shutterstock.com, p. 31.

Front cover: © Calyx22/Dreamstime.com.

Main body text set in Johann Light 30/36.